New
Hampshire

Mount Chocorua

New

Hampshire

Text and photographs by

Frederick John Pratson

The Stephen Greene Press

BRATTLEBORO, VERMONT

White Mountains, looking south

This book has been produced in the United
States of America: designed by R. L. Dothard
Associates, composed by American Book–
Stratford Press, printed by the Murray Print-
ing Company.

Pratson, Frederick John
  New Hampshire
  1. New Hampshire—Description and travel
—1951—Views.
F35.P72 1974   917.42′04′40222   73–86034
ISBN 0–8289–0206–2
ISBN 0–8289–0207–0 (pbk.)

Lake Winnipesaukee

Dedicated to:

My good friend Mrs. Bobbie Holbrook, of Fitzwilliam, and in fond memory of her late husband, Chief Donald Holbrook, financier, international fire protection expert, and extraordinary human being.

Other books by
Frederick John Pratson:

Land of the Four Directions
The Sea in Their Blood
The Special World of the Artisan
A Guide to Atlantic Canada

Introduction

MY FIRST EXPERIENCE with New Hampshire was in the mid-1950's, as a counselor at Camp Jewell, a YMCA camp once located on Swanzey Lake. I can still recall vividly the beautiful farm country, the still-working textile mill, the pristine Congregational church, the covered bridge at West Swanzey crossing the Ashuelot River, the fine horses grazing on long, rich grasses, the magnificent skies above the lake at sunset. And I remember the fun times too—the weekly trips into Keene to "take in" a movie and have a hamburger at the Crystal Restaurant, a treat to last the whole week; the summer-stock production of "Bell, Book, and Candle" at a theater near by; the exhilaration of climbing Mount Monadnock with a string of kids of all sizes, shapes and colors trailing behind me. Then there was the day I got lost with a group of campers somewhere in the deep, cool forest near the camp—a tense time turned joyous as we found our way back to camp via old logging roads and marched onto the playing field singing *The Happy Wanderer,* while angry and worried officials searched the countryside for us anxiously.

The areas of West Swanzey, Swanzey Lake, Keene and Mount Monadnock still look the same to me, although many of the faces and voices have long since gone and many of the names are now forgotten. Since that summer at "Y" camp I have spent many days in New Hampshire and have explored just about every part of the state. But there are still a number of places I have yet to see and I hope this will always be so. I relish the chance for new experiences in this rewarding state.

I especially like the look of the small towns of New Hampshire. Architecturally, they are superb, with many elegant homes set on expansive lawns, shaded by great maples and elms, reflecting much of the traditional in New England architecture—an architecture, I believe, unmatched in taste or style by any other region of North America. And the towns of New Hampshire offer a super-abundance of it.

I even like the sounds of their names—Freedom, Bethlehem, Canterbury, Derry, Exeter, Fitzwilliam, Hancock, Jefferson, Littleton, Lee, Mason, Peterborough, Nottingham, Ossipee, Stratford, Tinkerville, and Wentworth. These are sounds that are good to hear.

The charm and character of New Hampshire's small towns are enhanced by the diversity of its rich landscape. On countless trips throughout the state I have explored its mountains, rolling hills, rivers, streams, forests, meadows, marshes, seacoast and lakes. I recall with special pleasure the sight of the mist rising from a meadow or lake in the early morning, the smell and feel of freshly plowed farm land, the flashing image of a white-tail deer or trout caught unexpectedly in flight or frolic, or perhaps coming upon a beaver lodge deep in a White Mountains woods, the powerful surge of white water, the light green ferns superimposed over the darkness of surrounding brush, the joyful glow of Indian Paintbrush blooms bobbing in the breeze, the blaze of autumn, the freedom of running a ski trail after a newly fallen snow.

Perhaps even more than its towns and landscapes I admire the people of New Hampshire. They are hard-working, honest people, relying more on themselves than on the state and with, by and large, a strong belief in God, America, and in themselves. They can also be stubborn as mules: they are not easily pushed around by either their own or by outsiders. These are qualities they share with most of the rest of northern New England, with the people of Maine and Vermont, and are qualities to admire, and perhaps at no time more than now.

This portrait is my statement on New Hampshire, one of deep, personal affection.

FREDERICK JOHN PRATSON
North Scituate, 1974

9

Rye Beach

The Essence

NEW HAMPSHIRE is a place that reminds one of home, whether real or imagined. The small towns with their main streets, squares, white churches, picket fences and Civil War memorials; the people and their surroundings like Norman Rockwell paintings come to life—all make it easy to close your eyes and imagine yourself in the nineteenth-century America of "The Music Man," or "Our Town." And there are many times when this image of America, in New Hampshire, is real. Fleeting moments, spent in an off-the-main-road village with its honest people who still find amusement in simple pleasures, such as church socials and country fairs, express something of the best part of New Hampshire and of America—its innocence and its good nature.

People still help each other and take care of themselves in New Hampshire. They are laconic, suspicious and stubborn and also the opposite of all that, when the right sentiments are touched. There is a sense of deep roots about New Hampshire people, giving the strong impression that they have been there for ages and will continue to be there for a long time to come. The Tuttle family, for example, has been farming the same land, in Dover, for over 350 years. Theirs is the oldest family farm in America, with new generations coming along to keep it that way.

New Hampshire is a lamb-chop-shaped state, wedged between Vermont on the west and Maine on the east. To the south is Massachusetts and to the north the Canadian border, at the Province of Quebec. Its terrain is the most varied and monumental in all of New England. It has the tallest mountains in the eastern

*Daniel Webster
at State House*

United States, one of the largest lakes, a seacoast, deep forests, long rivers and gentle, rolling farmland.

The state comes into its glory in the fall when the harvest is in and the foliage turns into a blaze of reds, oranges and yellows. Soon after this colorful display winter creates a magical white and silver world of snow, frost and ice, firing the passions of skiers, dog-team masters, ice fishermen and snowmobilers. Spring in New Hampshire is a time of sugar maples, budding trees, sweet meadow smells and open trout streams. And summer is a lush green time when every aspect of the state's natural surroundings—the forests, lakes, sea and mountains—cleanse and relax the spirit.

It is a state of trim, lovely villages and red-bricked industrial cities. Its people —now nearly a million in number—come from all over the world, but are mainly old-time Yankee and of French-Canadian descent. New Hampshire-ites—both native and adopted—are known in all fields of endeavor. They have created myths (Thornton Wilder), religions (Mary Baker Eddy), and great works of art (Augustus Saint-Gaudens). And one of New Hampshire's native sons, Admiral Alan Shepard, was the first American in space and one of the first to explore the surface of the moon.

New Hampshire is rich in history. The state was the ninth of the original thirteen to enter the Union and some of its communities have already celebrated their 350th birthday.

The Industrial Revolution substantially changed a good part of New Hampshire from the almost totally agricultural region it was to an industrial state. Textile manufacturing became, and still is in many communities, the major economic force. Textile mills sprang up on fast-flowing rivers and estuaries, such as the Merrimac and the Piscataqua.

In addition to increasing the state's wealth, the thriving mills also expanded its population, both in numbers and in diversity. Prior to the mid-1880's, the people of New Hampshire were predominantly of Anglo-Saxon stock. Protestantism—chiefly Episcopal and Congregational—provided the people with spiritual solace and an uncompromising earthly ethic. These people were among the original New England Yankees.

With the need for more labor for the textile mills, new people from Quebec, Scotland and other European countries came into the state. In addition to contributing their sweat and muscle to New Hampshire's economy, they brought with them their rich cultures, in the form of varied languages, religions and traditions.

Both Yankee and immigrant worked long, hard hours in the mills, such as the famous seemingly-mile-long Amoskeag Mills. Far from letting their spirits be broken, the industrial people of New Hampshire prospered from their labors, not necessarily in monetary wealth but certainly in the richness of their own personal ethic.

The new immigrants settled primarily in or near the large cities, such as Nashua, Manchester, and Berlin. The French Canadians among them established their own churches, schools, religious orders, and hospitals. In fact, today, people of French-Canadian background form the largest ethnic group in the state, and the largest segment of the population of Manchester, New Hampshire's largest city. And, though suspicions caused by religious and cultural differences still linger in New Hampshire, they do not much interfere with the people's workaday efforts to improve their quality of life.

The basic philosophy of New Hampshire is conservative, religious, patriotic and provincial, often reflecting Thomas Jefferson's utopian vision of rugged

Connecticut River farm

17

Hillsboro County barn

self-reliance based on land ownership. John Stark, the hero of the Battle of Bennington (Vermont), gave the state its motto, "Live Free or Die." Even one of its loveliest towns is named Freedom.

This rugged individualism is reflected in its politics. Although the state is basically Republican, Democrats often win. And those that do—Republican and Democrat alike—are often the most interesting candidates, especially in the early presidential primary races. New Hampshire's "first in the nation" primary usually sets the trend for the rest of America by boosting the chances of the winner to earn his party's nomination. In recent years, John Kennedy, Richard Nixon, Eugene McCarthy and George McGovern have won their party's primary in New Hampshire. Kennedy and Nixon became presidents, McGovern won the Democratic nomination. McCarthy broke the pattern, he became a poet.

Politicians have learned not to take the people of New Hampshire for granted. McGovern, for one, won the primary but lost the state, in the general election, to Nixon. Edmund Muskie, a next-door neighbor from Maine, was beaten in his bid for the presidency when the voters turned thumbs down after his now famous speech in front of the *Manchester Union Leader* building.

Even the size of the New Hampshire legislature is somewhat a testament to the philosophical independence of New Hampshire-ites. It is the largest state legislature in the country, some citizens complaining that so many politicians is a waste while others feel the present system brings the government closer to the people by making each legislator more responsible to his constituents.

New Hampshire is a place rich in culture. Dartmouth, Exeter, St. Paul's, the University of New Hampshire, Franconia College, New England College, Franklin Pierce College, St. Anselm's College, Rivier College, Colby College, Mount Saint Mary College and several other institutions of high academic learn-

Jackson

ing form the backbone of the state's cultural life, and serve to balance its basic conservatism with inquiry, experimentation, and creativity in all fields. Students and faculty from throughout the world come to these New Hampshire institutions to learn and to teach. Some, in turn, contribute their energies, talents and new ideas to New Hampshire and the vast world beyond its borders.

One of the last places one would think to go to see a mural by a Mexican artist and revolutionary would be New Hampshire. Yet, in Dartmouth's Baker Library one can see just such a mural. There the struggles of the masses and their victory over their exploiters are depicted in a dramatic fresco painted by José Clemente Orozco. Just south of the Dartmouth campus, in Cornish, is located the former home and studio of one of America's most famous sculptors, Augustus Saint-Gaudens, now a memorial.

Near the beautiful town of Peterborough is the MacDowell Colony, a secluded retreat for artists, musicians, and writers. It was while staying at Mac-Dowell that Thornton Wilder was inspired to write the popular play, "Our Town," which is based at least partly on his impressions of New Hampshire village life. And the founder of the Christian Science religion, Mrs. Mary Baker Eddy, was born on the outskirts of Concord, New Hampshire's capital city.

Another outcropping of New Hampshire's varied culture is its fine architecture. The state's eighteenth-century and nineteenth-century architecture is splendid and often found in the most surprising places, such as a small village tucked far away from the main stream or a barn which looks more like an immense mansion. The city of Portsmouth is considered by many the most architecturally beautiful in New England. There are few contemporary buildings. Here one finds the John Paul Jones house, the Wentworth-Coolidge mansion and Strawberry Banke, a prized area of restored historical homes. Daniel Webster's birthplace, for one, was taken from its original site near

Hancock

23   *Hancock*

West Swanzey

Jaffrey

Franklin and is now one of the choice exhibits at Strawberry Banke.

The foregoing is not to say that New Hampshire is an *ideal* place. In many respects, it is. However, it also has its problems. It is one of the fastest growing states in the Union, in terms of both population and industrial expansion, and sees at first hand all the difficulties this implies.

Most of the growth is occurring in the southern region, in the Nashua, Manchester and Salem areas. Nashua, for example, has become an important electronics center. In addition, the tax environment in nearby Massachusetts has forced thousands of Massachusetts citizens across the border to take up residence in financially less-oppressive New Hampshire.

At the same time, in the central and northern regions, land and leisure home developers are dotting the magnificent landscape with vacation chalets and exclusive resorts. Hot dog, hamburger and french-fry stands are everywhere, far outnumbering the gracious restaurants, where food was once an experience and the ambiance was of home. There are more and more lackluster motels and fewer and fewer of the comfortable old-fashioned inns and the friendly respite they promised.

Some New Hampshire companies still pollute the once clear rivers while some ill-mannered residents and visitors continue to dirty the beautiful countryside. Increased taxation to pay for municipal services stimulated by the state's unprecedented growth is probably inevitable and will come as a shock, especially to those who sought New Hampshire as a last refuge. But the problems New Hampshire faces are not unique: they are the symptoms of "progress."

New Hampshire, as we have seen, abuts Vermont and Maine and is considered their sister state. But, unlike its sisters, New Hampshire conveys no instant mystique, such as the eighteenth-century rural Americana quality of Vermont or the Downeast salty seacoast aura of Maine. But New Hampshire does have a mystique that is perhaps more subtly powerful than that of either Vermont or Maine. This can best be seen in such works as "Our Town" and "The Devil and Daniel Webster." For through these works—and their reflection of the day-to-day struggle of so many to meet hardship and "the forces of evil" with a down-home pragmatic wile—the New Hampshire ethic becomes the New Hampshire mystique.

Lake Winnipesaukee

Start of dog sled race at Laconia

28

Sherman Adams, Lincoln

Mrs. Donald Holbrook, Fitzwilliam

Loon Mountain

Ossipee

Loon Mountain

The William Nichols family, Littleton

Selden Hannah,
Franconia

A Blessed Landscape

NEW HAMPSHIRE has been blessed by the forces of nature. It has a little bit of almost everything and a generous portion of some. New Hampshire has the most magnificent mountain range on the eastern portion of the North American continent. Even the Canadian Shield and the mountains of Cape Breton Island and Newfoundland cannot compare in rugged beauty and height to the White Mountains of New Hampshire. In fact, one would have to travel to the Rockies of the western United States and Canada to find mountains that are more impressive than those in New Hampshire. The White Mountain region reminds many people of the Alps in Switzerland. And to be sure North Conway in the winter skiing season does resemble a Swiss canton.

The White Mountains are actually part of the Appalachian chain, which shapes the land from northern Georgia to the Gaspé in the outer reaches of Quebec. The loftiest peak is the 6,288-foot-high Mount Washington, located in the Presidential Range of the White Mountains. Mount Washington is the tallest mountain in eastern North America, and one of the deadliest in the world. On a fair-weather day, during the summer, one can hike or drive a car to the top, or ride aboard a steam-engine train that chugs up a cogged-rail bed. But the weather on Mount Washington is unpredictable, seemingly changing from placid to fierce in the space of a few moments. Winds of over 230 miles an hour have been recorded there, and winds over 100 miles per hour are not unusual. Each year thousands of hikers and mountain climbers take on the challenges of Mount Washington and nearby peaks. And almost every year someone is killed in the attempt.

View from Bretton Woods

Atop Mount Washington

Relay equipment on Mount Washington

Twin Mountain

Old Man of the Mountains
Franconia Notch

White Mountains, looking south

The Appalachian Trail, a famous hiking trail that runs from the center of Maine to northern Georgia, passes through the White Mountains at Mount Washington, and the Appalachian Mountain Club, one of the oldest and best known outdoor organizations in America, has its New Hampshire headquarters in Pinkham Notch, at Mount Washington's base. The club maintains trails and camp sites for hikers and mountain climbers throughout the Presidential Range and its Pinkham Notch facility is the starting point for many expeditions on Mount Washington.

Tuckerman's Ravine, a steep bowl-shaped area on Mount Washington, can have snow until late May and sometimes even into early June. In most years it offers the last chance for skiing in the east before the start of summer. Fanatic skiers from throughout the United States and Canada come to Tuckerman's during this late season for one or two last exciting downhill runs. There are no tows and the only way to Tuckerman's jumping-off points is to trudge up the steep, snow-clad slopes on one's own feet.

Access through the White Mountains (an area officially called the White Mountain National Forest) can be gained through Crawford and Franconia Notches, as well as through Pinkham Notch. At Franconia Notch one can find such famous natural attractions as the Old Man of the Mountains (the state's best known symbol) and the Flume, a series of beautiful cascading waterfalls, and the Cannon Mountain ski area, with its spectacular Aerial Tramway. The granite profile of the Old Man of the Mountains seems to come alive when cloudy mists swirl around its rocky ledges, giving the craggy face an air of mystery rather as if some giant ancient human being had been forever imprisoned in stone by angry gods.

At the northern end of Crawford Notch is the start of the cog railway and the resort town of Bretton Woods. It was at Bretton Woods, several decades ago, that bankers from various of the world's leading nations met to work out a new monetary system. Their policies helped to pump new life into the war-torn nations of Europe.

The mountain scenery surrounding these three Notches is magnificent, with awesome stone walls rising through and beyond the clouds. The drive up the road that leads to the summit of Mount Washington is an experience not to be forgotten. At first, there is the womb-like envelopment of maples, oaks, and evergreens. Then, almost without warning, the road opens out of the trees giving the driver the eery perspective that the road has vanished, leaving the car moving rapidly toward outer space. It is an almost paralyzing sensation of shock which remains with one the rest of the way to the top. At the summit is a weather station manned throughout the year by individuals who seem at home with a nature that often goes berserk. From the summit, on a clear day, one can see Vermont, Maine, Massachusetts, the Atlantic Ocean, and Canada—a breathtaking panorama.

To the north of Mount Washington is the paper and pulp city of Berlin, with a population that is almost entirely of French-Canadian descent. The Androscoggin River flows through this part of the state from its source, Lake Umbagog, which is half in New Hampshire and half in Maine.

Much further to the north are the Connecticut Lakes and Lake Francis, all of which provide the starting waters for New England's most important river, the Connecticut. As the Connecticut flows south it serves to separate New Hampshire from Vermont, then cuts through the Pioneer Valley of Massachusetts, and through the center of the state of Connecticut, before emptying into Long Island Sound, at the town of Old Saybrook.

Some distance south of the Connecticut Lakes on the river is the town of

41

Connecticut River bridge linking Cornish, N.H. and Windsor, Vt.

Jackson

Old Fort No. 4, Charlestown

Orford

Orozco mural, Baker Library, Dartmouth College

Dartmouth Hall, Dartmouth College

Phillips Exeter Academy

Saint-Gaudens Memorial, Cornish

Orford, often a pleasant surprise to the unsuspecting traveller. For Orford has one of the most impressive rows of Bulfinch-style mansions in New England, set in spacious lawns and ornamented by stately trees and long white fences.

Just below Orford on the river is the town of Hanover, the site of Dartmouth College. Dartmouth was originally founded in the 1700's as a school for American Indian boys. However, after its early beginnings in this direction, it was not until recently that Dartmouth made a serious attempt at enrolling Indians. Nonetheless, Dartmouth has developed into one of the nation's outstanding academic institutions, in terms of scholarship, research, and the contributions made by its graduates. And Dartmouth is more than a bookish school. The mountainous landscape of New Hampshire makes skiers, hikers, and climbers out of even the most hard-nosed, city-oriented student.

South of Hanover, and also near the Connecticut River, is the former home and studio of the sculptor Augustus Saint-Gaudens. It is a memorial now and bits and pieces of statues can still be seen through the workshop windows. The estate is secluded from the main road and has a serenity that must have been ideal for the spiritual and creative mind. A little further south, and east of Claremont, are Lake and Mount Sunapee. In addition to being a popular skiing area, Mount Sunapee is the scene of an annual crafts fair, where potters, weavers, wood-carvers, leather-workers and other artisans show their wares and demonstrate their talents. And south of Sunapee, in towns like Alstead and Acworth, is maple-sugar country. There the trees are tapped in early spring, when the days are warm and the nights still cold. The sap is then boiled down into a thick, rich, delicious syrup which delights one's taste buds.

Keene, dominated by the singular 3,165-foot-high Mount Monadnock, is the largest city in southwestern New Hampshire. Its Main Street is one of the broadest in the nation, culminating at a circular green. Near Mount Monadnock, one of New Hampshire's geological prizes, are some of the loveliest of all New Hampshire towns—West Swanzey, Fitzwilliam, Jaffrey, Dublin, Hancock, and Troy. It was at Fitzwilliam that a Boston financeer created, with his own money, leadership and talents, one of the finest county volunteer fire departments in America. He named it after his Fitzwilliam estate, Meadowood. It, like the other volunteer fire departments of New Hampshire, is strong in the American tradition of people helping their neighbors when they are in need and in joining together for a good time when no emergency is at hand.

In the town of Dublin is the headquarters of one of the most interesting publishing enterprises in the nation—a five-pronged venture including *Yankee* magazine, the *Old Farmer's Almanac, New England Guide, Cape Cod Compass* and *The New Englander*. Near by, at Rindge, is the world-famous non-denominational religious shrine, the Cathedral of the Pines. This lovely natural cathedral is what a place of worship should be. Its roof is the sky, arched by tall pine trees; its altar a lake, a forest and the silhouette of Mount Monadnock; and its spirit one of universal brotherhood. Just up the road a bit, north of Peterborough, is the Crotched Mountain Rehabilitation Center. The center is located on a high hill overlooking a broad valley. It is a place of real hope for children who have not been favored with the healthy bodies most of us take for granted.

Further east, right next door to the thriving industrial city of Nashua in Hudson, is New England's best zoo, Benson's Wild Animal Farm, where one can see pythons, lions, bears, tigers, elephants, monkeys and many other species of wildlife. This is a private operation that plows back enough of its revenues to keep the park beautiful, exciting and interesting for all ages and to make animal watching a pleasure instead of the pain of conscience it sometimes is. Another

53

Mount Monadnock

White Mountains, looking east

South Acworth

56

West Swanzey

Fitzwilliam

59

Hancock

Mrs. Frank Massin

Charles Wallace, proprietor of the Fitzwilliam Inn

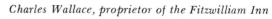

Judson Hale, editor of Yankee,
in front of portrait of
founder Robb Sagendorph

Below, Mount Washington
Cogged Railway engineer

WAUMBEK

Cathedral of the Pines, Rindge

Opposite: left, Little Harbor Chapel, Portsmouth;
right, Old Meeting House, Jaffrey

Dog sled run near Laconia

Rindge

20 miles or so on near the town of Salem is Mystery Hill, a collection of stones that some believe were assembled by Vikings or other Europeans who might have explored this section of the state about a thousand years ago. One might well call Mystery Hill New England's Stonehenge.

To the north of Nashua and Salem are the cities of Manchester and Concord. Manchester has a few tall, modern buildings, good evidence of its emergence out of its textile past and into the space age. However, the long red-brick mills and the company row-houses are still there. While they are relics of the past, one which some people would like to forget, these structures should be preserved—for their beauty and because America sorely needs to conserve all the reminders of its rich heritage it can.

The main business of Concord is government. The gold dome of the State House is the gleaming focal point of the city. There are two statues in the park in front of the State House, one of Daniel Webster and the other of General John Stark, representing some of the best of New Hampshire's traditions. Many decades ago, Concord was the Detroit of America, producing hundreds of stage coaches each year. The Concord Coach was well known to both the sophisticated traveller and to the masked highwayman.

Not far from Concord is the lovely rural community of Canterbury. Canterbury is the location of a Shaker village. Almost all of the Shaker inhabitants have died out but the grounds, buildings and artifacts of their utopian society can still be seen in Canterbury. The Shakers were one of the most self-reliant and enterprising groups of people to settle in New Hampshire, as well as in other parts of New England and New York State. The simplicity, efficiency and purity of their furniture design is known throughout the world both for itself and as the basis from which much modern design developed. The Shaker religion worked beautifully in terms of providing spiritual joy and earthly accommodation to its followers, but failed to survive because it forebade physical love and its resultant regeneration.

To the east of Manchester and Concord are the academic towns of Exeter and Durham. The sprawling Georgian campus of the University of New Hampshire is in Durham. The most stunning contemporary buildings in the entire state are those of the New England Center for Continuing Education, which is an entity of the University. These massive buildings are designed to blend with the surrounding tall pines to such a degree as to seem an integral element of nature.

Phillips Exeter Academy is in the town of Exeter and is one of America's most prestigious prep schools, with many of its graduates going on to "Ivy League" universities, such as Harvard, Yale and Princeton. And it was on a lonely road near the town of Exeter, one night in 1965, that a couple out driving claim to have been captured and interrogated by creatures from outer space soon after they witnessed the landing of a flying saucer.

Between Durham and Exeter is the Great Bay, a large salt water lake, which is fed from the sea via the Piscataqua estuary. Near Great Bay is the lovely city of Portsmouth and the New Hampshire seacoast on the Atlantic Ocean. Portsmouth is home to the Portsmouth Naval Base where submarines and other vessels are built for the United States Navy, and where such famous ships as the *Raleigh* and *Ranger,* of Revolutionary fame, were once built. One of the finest buildings in the Portsmouth area is the Wentworth-Coolidge mansion, once belonging to a governor of the state and later to a Boston Brahmin. Portsmouth itself is a treasure box of beautiful mansions. Its Strawberry Banke restorations of historic New Hampshire buildings and their interior furnishings, as well as demonstrations of how life was lived in past centuries, are a most important contribution to the preservation of America's historic heritage.

67

Benson's Wild Animal Farm, Hudson

69

North Conway railway station

Newmarket mill

71

Ice fishing shanties and, below, boys fishing on Lake Opeechee

Canterbury

77

Shaker Village house, Canterbury

*Governor Langdon house and
graveyard, Portsmouth*

Weaving display, Strawberry Banke, Portsmouth

Peirce Mansion, Portsmouth

Strawberry Banke

Strawberry Banke

The seacoast of New Hampshire is very short in comparison to that of Maine or Massachusetts—even little Rhode Island has more. But there is enough of it to give people a feeling of the everlasting sea. Seabrook, Rye, and Hampton are the main shore towns. Hampton Beach is well known throughout eastern United States and Canada for its good beaches, accommodations, and recreation. In the summer, Hampton's sand and surf area is mobbed with bronzed, bikini-clad sun and sea worshipers. The tightly packed-together curio shops, restaurants, and tourist lodgings form a colorful quilt of varying shapes, hues, and textures. The smells of frying onions, pizzas, hot dogs and hamburgers are not those of *haute cuisine* but powerful enough to overwhelm appetites already sharpened by the salt air.

The Rye Beach area is more proper and established, with fine mansions and resorts overlooking the blue Atlantic waters. Fishermen and lobstermen still sail out of Rye and give the town a workaday quality, keeping it from seeming too pretentious. In the distance one can see the forms and the lighthouse of the Isles of Shoals. The Isles of Shoals are in both New Hampshire and Maine waters and both states claim them, often causing bitterness on all sides.

One of New England's largest and most beautiful fresh water lakes, Lake Winnipesaukee, is located northwest and inland of Portsmouth. This lovely lake is ranked, with the White Mountains and the seacoast, as being one of the state's most important recreational areas. Lake Winnipesaukee is surrounded by the resort communities of Weirs, Gilford, Alton, Wolfeboro, Moultonborough, Center Harbor, and Meredith. During the winter, championship dog-sled races take place in nearby Laconia, snowmobiling on the grounds of the Castle in the Clouds at Moultonborough, and ice fishing anywhere there's firm water. And in the summer, large vessels, such as the *Mount Washington,* and others, cruise the lake, allowing people a restful opportunity to enjoy the beautiful scenery and stimulating air.

Somewhat northwest of Lake Winnipesaukee on the way to Conway is Lake Chocorua and the 3,475-foot-high Mount Chocorua. Mount Chocorua, rising magestically as it does at the far end of Lake Chocorua, is probably the single most attractive sight in New Hampshire. While the high peaks of the Presidential Range often seem beyond human comprehension, Mount Chocorua—through its single loveliness and the harmonious relationship of the mountain, the lake and the surrounding leaning birches—allows one to focus on the simple magnificence of the natural world and promotes a serenity too seldom found.

At a point between Mount Chocorua and the town of Conway is the entrance to the very scenic Kancamagus Highway, which runs to Loon Mountain ski area and the town of Lincoln. White water rivers, mountain vistas, and hiking trails make the Kancamagus Highway a most pleasant route through the rich natural beauty of the southern portion of the White Mountain National Forest. Along this highway are stands of white birches that rival the famous Shelburne birches further northeast near Gorham. At the end of the highway and to the west of Lincoln, and almost back to Franconia, is the appealing Lost River and Kinsman Notch area, and so the circle closes.

These, then, are the highlights of some of the key places in New Hampshire. But the real joy to be had in New Hampshire lies in discovering the towns, the history, the covered bridges, the architectural gems, and the choice natural spots by one's self, or with a good friend. Often the best experiences come as a surprise, around the bend of a dirt road or on a woodland trail. Suddenly the world unfolds in a new and better way, and one senses a powerful urge to stay there forever to savor the feeling of peace and harmony.

83

Rye Beach estuary

Hampton Beach area

Seabrook

89

Rye Beach

A Place of Peace

THE INDEPENDENT and resourceful spirit and blessed landscape are not all one encounters in New Hampshire. The long, dull highways, crammed with combustion-powered tin cans are also to be found. And so are the billboards, greasy eateries, made-in-Hong-Kong come-ons, and the slick hucksters. But tranquility does exist in great abundance in New Hampshire. You can find it in Jackson, Littleton, Mason, Freedom, Ossipee, West Rye, Stoddard, Tamworth, Derry, Dover, New London, and dozens of other places.

The lush greens of summer, the hot colors of autumn, the ice purples and whites of winter, and the pastels of spring are used by nature to paint a different picture of New Hampshire each season. The sounds of wind, white water, surf, tumbling rocks, thunder, song birds, owls, cows, tractors, falling timber, and insects of the night create an ever-changing music. And the dead silence of a cold winter's evening, accented by the faint scent of burning cedar logs floating from some distant chimney, makes the world seem, if only fleetingly, one's own

exclusive domain. The glorious surge of self importance felt atop a Mount Washington and the humbling insignificance felt trudging up from its base force an acute awareness of living, not merely existing. All this, too, is New Hampshire.

Most visitors come to New Hampshire to have a good time. And it offers much of that. There is great fresh and salt water swimming, skiing, hiking, sight-seeing and fall-foliage-touring, camping, boating, and the chance simply to relax in fresh, clean air and beautiful countryside. But New Hampshire is a great deal more than just a vacation, a retreat for the wealthy and the famous, or a grand social event. New Hampshire, at its best, is what America, at its best, is all about—self-reliance, rugged individualism, neighborliness, love of liberty, deep religious conviction, a close communion with the natural world, and a desire for peace.

Canterbury countryside

Glen Ellis

94

Glen Ellis

Lake Chocorua

96